WOMEN AT A
CROSSROADS

A Travel Guide — Destination Vote

WOMAN'S
LIBERTY BELL
JUSTICE
EQUALITY
1915
PENNSYLVANIA

WOMEN AT A CROSSROADS

A Travel Guide — Destination Vote

poetry by
JEN SCHNEIDER

SHANTI ARTS PUBLISHING

BRUNSWICK, MAINE

Women at a Crossroads:
A Travel Guide — Destination Vote

Published by Shanti Arts Publishing

Designed by Shanti Arts Designs

Images— COVER [top] Harris & Ewing, photographer, Suffrage Picket Parade, 1917. United States Library of Congress. https://cdn.loc.gov/service/pnp/hec/10300/10337v.jpg; [middle] Harris & Ewing, photographer, Suffrage Picket Parade, 1917. United States Library of Congress; [bottom] Bain News Service, Suffragists who took part in the Suffrage Hike from New York City to Washington, D.C., 1913. United States Library of Congress. http://hdl.loc.gov/loc.pnp/ggbain.11476. TITLE PAGE Woman's Liberty Bell, Justice Equality 1915 Pennsylvania Pin. Wikimedia Commons.

Shanti Arts LLC
193 Hillside Road
Brunswick, Maine 04011

shantiarts.com

Printed in the United States of America

ISBN: 978-1-962082-60-0 (softcover)

Library of Congress Control Number: 2025934582

Dedicated to

women named ____

> *crossroads*
> *direction*
> *disruption*
> *steps taken*
> *steps to be had*
>
> *mentors*
> *guides*
> *far-fetched notions*
> *persistent potions*
> *and their many forms*

my head's free at last

alarm in another moment
nowhere to be found
how is it I can't see you

       a little shaking
       no chance
       delighted
       succeeded

       a graceful zigzag

among the leaves
with _ wings

roots of trees
banks
hedges

       pleasing !

Contents

Acknowledgments

Black Stone / White Stone: "'Advice from a Caterpillar' (on freedom)" (Summer 2024)

Feral Journal: "10 (Plus) Ways to Fuel and Feed a Hunger" (Summer/Fall 2022)

Fevers of the Mind: "of hands and handiwork :: a woman named ____" (October 2022)

International Women's Day Anthology 2022, Moonstone Arts Center: "my head's free at last"

Not Ghosts, But Spirits—Volume II, Querencia Press: "a poem about the flight and fight to win the right to vote for women / on suffrage, seeds, and stuff"

The Nuances of New-Age Feminism, Musing Publications: "some say she doth ____ too much :: on forms (and performances) of speech" (September 2022)

The Philadelphia Lawyer: "A Woman Named Arabella" (Spring 2023)

Querencia Press's Winter 2023 Anthology: "a poem about the flight and fight to win the right to vote for women / on suffrage, seeds, and stuff"

Spillwords: "Women at a Crossroads: 20 (plus) Ways to Disrupt a Timeline" (April 2023)

Struggle for Liberty Anthology 2022, Moonstone Arts Center: "on defining a movement :: of freedom and liberty"

Voidspace Zine: "20 (plus) ways to thread a knot (and cross-stitch)"; "Anatomy of a Shirtwaist" (August 2022); and "A Bingo Board Reflection on International Women's Day (IWD)" (April 2023)

He who knows one, knows none.

—Max Müller

We do not escape into philosophy, psychology, and art—
we go there to restore our shattered selves into whole ones.

—Anaïs Nin

How to Get There (Origins)

I do not believe that women are better than men.
We have not wrecked railroads, nor corrupted legislature,
nor done many unholy things that men have done;
but then we must remember
that we have not had the chance.

—Jane Addams

on defining a movement :: of freedom and liberty

a woman named judith
knew that there is no one way
to define a movement / or a destiny

> *I believed in suffrage*
> *before there was such a word*
> *in the dictionary*

a member / of the suffrage
movement from inception
to celebration to continuation

of bird calls
and callings / sunflowers
and blue tin signs
/ of corsets and customs
purple, white, and gold
rainbows / saucy recipes
and reciprocity

judith winsor smith
imagined a state of freedom
and liberty / a concept
termed suffrage / long before
the word was either coined
or codified in dictionary form

a woman named judith
knew that there is no one way
to define a movement
/ a destiny—grounded in paths
to pave / and rights to reconcile

20 (plus) ways to thread a knot (and cross-stitch)

1. a means of survival :: to sew
2. a source of sustenance :: boarders
3. Mother Winifred served as a garment :: worker
4. to support Leonora and a younger :: brother
5. Father John, a :: printer
6. also a member of The Knights of :: Labor
7. Leonora left school at age :: eleven
8. for a post as a :: seamstress
9. born in :: New York State
10. on the sixteenth day of :: February
11. date of death, April :: Third
12. a woman named :: Leonora
13. stitched strands of fiber and :: syllables
14. to thread ties between :: classes
15. working and :: middle
16. an advocate for working :: women
17. an organizer of :: protesters
18. at home in factories and industrial :: schools
19. a creator of shirtwaists and sewing room :: cooperatives
20. a leader of movements, settlement :: house
21. a force in the women's trade union :: league
22. a leading :: voice

a woman named Leonora
toiled of needles
and knowledge
that the past
need not knot
the future

each cell
/ a stitch

of 20,000
/ knots

a poem about the flight and fight to win the right to vote for women / on suffrage, seeds, and stuff

october :: dusk turns to dawn. calendar pages continue to cycle. aviary arrangements sprout (exponentially) in soil and sky. skies beam rays both gregarious and glorious. all hues a blend of mocha and happenstance. all months monitored. flocks in flight. broken wings ready to fly. miles to climb. miles and milestones rarely conquered in minutes (or moments). mates and dates tangle in autumn leaves. hues of crimson, chocolate, and kelly green vines dance with clovers of three (sometimes four) leaves. late nesters linger. mourning doves meander. all species industrious, multiple broods banter. autumn winds tango as souls in soles stir. march (1) both a moment and a state of being. advocacy and advocates nest (no time to rest) in nimble spaces. worms wonder and wander. inch by inch. ideas rustle in small pockets of air.

migration a cycle of moments turned minutes turned memories

january :: broods and broads battle winter winds. limbs lock in layers. flannels and feathers spread heat and traction (amidst multiple factions). stray branches sag then settle. snow and snowy doves accumulate inches and inklings. icy stares battle household wares. flocks follow land (destinations ripe with anticipation). migration routes make room for movers and makers. instincts and imaginations trace tracks and new trails. species both sapiens and feathered funnel (and flock) areas and avenues (2) of aspiration and inspiration. spherical lens travel distances both documented and undeclared. binoculars reveal patterns of primed propositions. all prepositions inked. all feather (and fonts) focused. brea(d)th reveals lines (often well defined) of life and limits.

music a migration of curiosities turned chirps turned cycles

march :: baby chicks are born with wings in fetal positions. all feathers combed. flaps and fledglings eager for food and flight. parades and propositions of paramount importance. all nests targets. parasites and predators persist. march winds / lion's roars / both a memory and a moment (3) limbs light with bounce. hops taken in stride. all gaits a gander. all gazes grounded. longer legs make for faster walking. all steps a blend of ideas stewed on a slow boil. puffs (breath both bated and weighted) simultaneously stoke travel and transgressions.

flight a symphony of notes turned north stars

april :: nests constructed of twig, twine, and time nurture. brush and bristles protect. persistence wrapped in paper dolls (dna linked across regions) and linen layers (needles and knots resemble patterns inked and linked in compilations). shadows linger. the vigilant seize victories. sized of varying containers (plastics on the horizon / paper puddles and pools). small and large gaits gain traction. all nests a process. all beaks a tool. all builds a beacon. foundations and flocks often fragments (and fragmented) of wind and wonder.

distance decorated of flight, food, and feathers

july :: planted seeds sprout. sticks tangle. symphonies conduct canopies of crushing beauty. rush hour a july sky. conductors wave wands of fire and ice. lightning chases thunder. asteroids and constellations clash. meters and meteorites gain attention. all senses engaged (some enraged). all birds blue (time and tin both chased and chasing transformation). young raised (4) in pre-existing nesting cavities. all wings ready for flight.

danger a dance of daisies, distance and destination

august :: efforts of june (turned july), and many moons (in perpetual rotation) (5) perform. all the world's a stage. advocacy as much art as aviation. cycles spin with carousels. all ponies freshly painted. all saddles taken. lyrics linger in air heavy of salt

and sauerkraut. four-legged mammals a loyal companion. barks
both warning and waning.

anger and danger a difference of a single degree turned letter

gregorian.calendars.cycle.curiosities.spin.carousels.turn.pages.
of.time.september.october.november.december,january.february.
march.april.may.june.july.august.september.the.gregorian.calendar.
both.divided.and.united.of.days.and.destinies.long.and.layered.all.
days.to.suffer.both.a.state.of.being.and.a.reason.to.be.more.than.
simply.to.be.gregorian.calendars.continue.to.cycle.spin.turn.

1. souls in rubber soles march (make) through / of history (1915)
2. march both a moment and a momentum
3. parade routes neither routine nor regulated (1913)
4. babes in never never land toy with prepositions and
   propositions
5. moons orbit earth / earth orbits sun / calendars cycle
   and spin / souls in rubber soles continue to march

Love Letter to the Girls Who'd Doodle
/ and Oodles of Questions I'd Like to Dabble

As a child, I'd spend hours scribbling in notebooks. Elders and
teachers would seize my doodles, stomp their boots, then claim I'd
had no right. I learned to reserve eight-and-a-half by eleven pages
for the small pockets of air between bed and night. Tick. Tock.
Time. Worth. Wonder. Thunder. Curious concepts. Nebulous
monitors. With all minutes clocked, I'd study—ABCs. Suffragists
named Abigail Scott Duniway, Ruth Law (quite a bird), Edith
Garrud (a Jiu-jitsu Queen), and Nina Allender, the cartoonist.
Like them and so many others, I never gave a hoot. Instead, I'd
take notes and make note. I'd doodle. Like Duniway.

On Duniway
they tell me what words may be spoken
and what questions may be asked
mostly fluff of tissues and dust

they reproduce their prejudice
they shoot the breeze
but the breeze (w)inks back

I disagree. I digress. I dress.

They fail to impress. I draw
the words I wish to see. Of birds.
And sparks. And uncoiffed locks.
Of svelte shapes. Of shapely waists.
Of impatiens. And impatience. Of patient waits.
Of fresh blooms. Of signs. Of changed
times. Of transparent stinks.

Simple strokes. Spill. Spell. Soil.
In ink. Of think. Suits in pinstriped-
cases blush then blink. They wink
They tattle. They fail to rattle.

We battle. New strokes. New blends.
New notes. Folks in floral dress clothes toil.
Fresh soil. New Votes.

Seventy years in states of germination.
A new nation.
Just. Like.
That.

The girls in the pages of my book sought a just right. Collected scraps. Swapped sparks. *To envision. To vote.* To stitch new coats. Freedoms—theirs, mine, knotted by time—were unlocked under covers of wool and nylon. Debates were endlessly covered. Not wanting to be discovered. Allender knew not to wait for Mr. Right. *Hello, Rights. Goodbye, Plights.* She sought a divorce when her husband fled in the night. He had gambled on funds and sought fun in far corners as Allender prioritized orders. *Dibble. Dabble. Doodle.* Sketch a novel proposition. Edit a new world order. Anticipate then generate ongoing revision.

The girls in the pages of my books taught ABCs, self-defense, flight, and the power of the pen to recreate might. Nina Allender drew. She sketched her own path and inked her own worth. The girl. The Allender Girl. Not perfect. As predictable as she was bold. Of svelte proportions. Young. Not old. Always white. *Why?* Of high fashion and high stakes. Rights on the line. Depicted in manners utterly sublime. Did she whitewash a vision or mind wash with good reason. Allender represented a freedom like that of my own doodles. Set sights on magazine covers and eons of foibles. She tossed aside visions of the staid and the frumpy. Forged an original image of the meaning of suffrage and society. She represented a claim to freedom. But failed to represent many. Headlines press. *Acknowledgment denied.* The doodles in my notebook had an uncanny similarity. The Allender Girl equally at fault. With her ink she erased as much as she sought. Many layers of and to liberation. The times rarely offered windows and lights. *Perhaps.* Of layers of lace and corsets neatly traced. Tightly tied. Her graphics graced covers of *The Suffragist* and transformed a nation. The galleries full of cartoons inked in black and white. The stories far less distinct. Much more blurred. Pastel blends by day. Sharp angles by night.

I wonder what they—Duniway, Garrud, Law, Allender, more— might think of today's marches and of our digital ink. Of Crockett Johnson's *Harold and the Purple Crayon*. Of Roald Dahl's books being rewritten. Of banned texts and artificial intelligence. Of *Roe v Wade*. Of *Dobbs v. Jackson Women's Health Organization*. Of *Obergefell v. Hodges*. Of Twitter and Capitol mobs. Of marches in pink. Mostly, of the ongoing fight. To protect a woman's rights.

On Nina Allender and (D)oodles of Questions I'd Like to Ask.

1. Did you have a favored color of ink?
2. Is purple the proper hue for the movement?
3. Can you describe the contents of your pencil case?
4. For your work—Why an unlabeled box stocked in an unopened closet?
5. If not Harold, then who?
6. What about Dobbs?
7. Of the over one hundred fifty political cartoons you inked for *The Suffragist*, did you have a favorite?
8. Why are all the figures white?
9. Do you recall your first draft?
10. Do you have any regrets?
11. Did you draw what you knew or what you wished could be?
12. Can you describe your creative process?
13. Which was harder, filing for divorce or filing your first cartoon with your editor?
14. Is the Allender Girl everything you had hoped for?
15. Do your cartoons depict truths or trials or both?
16. Of today's Supreme Court, do you harbor spite?
17. Do your cartoons reflect your roots?
18. Do your doodles reflect your hopes?

19. Name three things you most love.
20. If I asked you to draw a cartoon for today, what message might it convey?
21. Of men in boots, do you give a hoot?

Dear President Wilson,
I Wonder What You Think

In one hand,
the president holds

a fountain

pen, full
of self-contained ink,

and in the other,

a sandwich—bologna
on rye,

I think—

I don't ask, but
I'd like to

know

which one he references
when he looks us in the eye
and addresses the nation

cameras and reels
point
lasers and losses at
our shadows

on the street

I used a ballpoint,
newly designed,
to sketch

the words he's surely seen

"Mr. President"

Please

"we protest
against the continued
disenfranchisement of American women for
which the President of the United States is responsible"

"It is unthinkable
that a national government
which represents women should ignore
the issue of the right of all women to political freedom."

Signed—Lucy Burns,
            Co-Founder of the National Woman's Party

I do not take a seat.

I imagine he takes a bite, a large one,
from his slice of wonder. The bologna
seasoned with a splat of mustard.

            (prescient me—"Wonder" would
            once again hit the market on May
            21, 1921—two years after
            and sandwiched between
            the passage on June 4, 1919
            and ratification—August 18, 1920
            by Congress of Amendment Nineteen)
now, amidst
and amongst agitation
and protest—mine / ours

He

feeds his hunger.
fuels his need for power.

He

calls our actions sour.

It's not the way,

he says, to make a point. Disappointing.
Disgusting, in fact. Then wags his pen at dust
mites.
Dusk falls. Stop this fight. He takes another bite.

Just. Like. That.

We

do not Speak

We

stand in solidarity on concrete

The lawn behind our backs lush

The condemnation for our protests plush.

The air silent

The Silent Sentinels

Speak
Guards rush.

Mr. President,

>   We blink
>   We wonder
>   We think

We think you've missed the point—

You, this nation's 28th president

A resident
A leader
A self-proclaimed protector

Of troops
Of democracy
Of rights

"No one but the President,"

you say,

>   *wink*

"seems to be expected . . . to
look out for the general interests of the country."

Mr. President,

We wonder what you think
        of Amendment 19

We think you've missed the point—

Your fountain pen
has never been less on point

19 (plus) reasons to Wonder

1. Fountains persist in floodplains.
2. Not all floodplains fuse from land formations.
3. Ink pools in unexpected territories.
4. Self-contained ink was once revolutionary.
5. Bread holds as many meanings as flavors.
6. The ballpoint pen was patented in 1888.
7. Wonder hit the market in 1921.
8. Not all points are patentable.
9. Not all pens are self-contained.
10. Ink comes in a variety of hues.
11. Wink and Sink share all but one letter.
12. Progressiveness is a matter of perspective.
13. Neutrality is often a point of origin.
14. General interests typically lack seasons and seasoning.
15. Even sliced bread, including Wonder, spoils.
16. Sentinels protect what's waiting as much as watch for what's not.
17. Silent ink speaks with multiple forms of speech.
18. Prescient can serve both noun and verb.
19. Not all thoughts are thorough.
20. Nineteen is a prime number. Silence wonders.

Accommodations and Packing Lists

Woman will ride to emancipation and equal freedom
with man, full and complete, on a bicycle and in bloomers.

—"New Woman's Garb: Shall She Wear Bloomers
or Retain Her Skirts? Widespread Discussion of and
Deep Feelings Aroused by the Innovation," *New York Sun*, 1895

Anatomy of a Shirtwaist

1. Fabric, washed and :: ironed
2. Neatly :: pressed
3. Review, then lay out :: pattern
4. All pieces :: cut
5. Cotton thread :: ready
6. Fingers in :: check
7. Sew yoke to :: bodice
8. Ensure a looser :: fit
9. Inspect :: gathers
10. Prepare to attach :: collar
11. Handsewn :: closed
12. Sew interior of sleeve :: cuffs
13. Attach a :: waistband
14. Handsewn :: shut
15. Buttonholes up the :: back
16. Embellish collar with :: lace
17. And a vintage :: pin
18. No corners :: cut
19. Affix front :: fasteners
20. Finish interior :: seams
21. French or flat :: felled
22. Sometimes a stab and poke :: routine

> a garment
> both classy
> / and classless
>
> each cell
> / a stitch
>
> threaded
> of muscle
> / cotton fibers
>
> in preparation
> for an uprising
> / of 20000 knots

On Meeting Alice

Police stations are typically unfriendly. Thankfully, on the night I was arrested, the God my Irish-Catholic family sought watched over me.

I'd been sitting in a cell for nearly three hours. There were a variety of ways to describe my offense.

If you asked me, I was simply speaking the truth and explaining what should, what should be.

I'd been selling a newsletter titled *Votes for Women*, put out by the Women's Social and Political Union, an organization dedicated to fighting for women's rights in the United Kingdom.

Later, I joined a protest.

The officers said I was out of order.

I'd always been taught that order is relative.

But I digress. What matters is not that I was arrested, but that I was arrested at that corner and on that day.

It was lucky. It was life-changing. It was meant to be.

Another woman was also under duress.

Alice. It's how we met.

Mama would often say good things come in pairs.

Alice and I—we made a good pair.
I had spent the day in the square. Practicing. Perfecting my speech.
There were many of us. All tired. Officers on all corners.
"Stop," they'd say.

"Move right. Move left. This is not the way."

"What way, officer?" I asked. "Yours or mine."

"Enough," he said. And with that my hands were tied.

He pressed on my back. I heard a bone crack. The extra time I'd taken to tie my corset undeniably wasted.

In the station the air was cold.

The men consumed liverwurst sandwiches and ale. My stomach growled.

I was not alone. A woman sat head high on a nearby bench. She smiled.

"Hungry?" she asked.

"You bet."

"What for?"

"More."

"Always," she said.

"Quiet," interjected a guard.

"Excuse me," the woman countered. "We may not have the vote— yet—but we're allowed to speak."

"Don't push. Don't push too hard," the guard said.

"I shall," she replied.

He glared then shook the keys on his ring, as if we needed the reminder of the locked doors at our feet.

"Do as you please," he continued, "but don't forget what this means."

"Never," she said.

"Never," I agreed.

We both smiled. Our eyes tired. Even so, I felt inspired.

Turns out, anger boils more readily when not alone.

The oversized guard, unshaven and without cares, scribbled in an equally oversized leather-bound notebook. I couldn't make out what he wrote. His body spoke loudly, loudly enough. A mouse ran across the floor as his pen scratched.

The woman called to it. "Come!"

The guard looked up, and she pointed to the creature at his feet. He jumped. She laughed.

Both of us in the station because of our protests.
"I see an American flag pin on your lapel?"

"Yes Ma'am," I said while she continued to talk.

We shared similar concerns. We connected. Over pins. Of points.

One stitch. One thread. Goals. Forever aligned.

"I said quiet," the guard repeated as he stood. His legs planted. His brown eyes narrowed.

"Gotcha," she said then snapped. Just like that.

I snapped back. We began to speak, to speak in code.

Found ways to connect, ways the guard could never know.
We traded names.

A.L.I.C.E.

L.U.C.Y.

We compared end games.

T.H.E. V.O.T.E.

E.Q.U.A.L.I.T.Y.

We pledged.

F.R.I.E.N.D.S.

S.O.L.I.D.A.R.I.T.Y.

Stray Threads

overhea(r)d
at the printer's
press stocked
and stacked
in a structure
of worn
wools
and words
situated behind
the seamstress

How to Write a Right

line	by	line
each	stitch	a step
each	syllable	a form

of thyme

The Ad(dress)

curved	hems
curated	stems
seasonal	blooms
cyclical	looms
knit	purl
whirl	twirl
aprons	acronyms
corsets	clovers
measured	terms

destination	declined
goals	re(fine)d
subject to	imbalance
the dress	an awkward nest

the great (r)egret

a common bird
regularly found
of nests
and corsets
wings clipped

st(itches)

the
corset's stitch

—an itch
craving not
a scratch but an extra inch

sc(rat)ches

the straight stitch
most versatile, the zig-zag
least difficult to sow.

overlocks, buttonhole,
gathering, basting—
ready. set. sew.

NO
swap backtalk
for backstitches

trade cunning
for running stitches

sc(rat)ch   rats

st(itch)   itches

seize   rays   of   sun   in   st(ray)   threads

How to Dress a Suffragist (Pattern #1)

1. Loop laces on well-greased boots.
2. Water children, grass, men, and itches.
3. Redefine confined spaces.
4. Confine no waists. Confide without waste.
5. Fuel resolve with flavored notions.
6. Squelch stenches and trenched positions.
7. Reveal novel paths. Forgo traditional baths.
8. Parse subtexts for (sp)ice and story.
9. Stir strife. Sift (and lift) serendipity.
10. Appreciate the stickiness of cinnamon buns (and aprons).
11. Gift ideas in stripes and sashes.
12. Gather novelists. Refuse to grovel.
13. Filter philosophical fumes and wonderings.
14. Celebrate sonic divergence. Rally resistance.
15. Gather lose threads and wayward strands for knotting.
16. Balance all bow (and rip) ti(d)es.
17. Place ribbings (and ribbon) in proper places.
18. Welcome varied voices and variegated stitches.
19. Sooth (st)itches. Scratch (r)ashes.

How to Dress a Suffragist (Pattern #2)

1. Amend traditional hems and humming.
2. Tussle truths of varied seasons.
3. Pluck rips, tears, stares, and airs.
4. Bolt and brew tartan, gingham, and asymmetrical plaids.
5. Accept more variability, exclude less vocality.
6. Braise and raise preparations for informal runways.
7. Leave room, in waists and necklines, for multiple truths.
8. Prune necklines. Probe straight lines.
9. Drain (s)words from needles and looks untoward.
10. Dip fabrics in hues beyond the rainbow.
11. Clip lips of drips. Swipe gripes with wipes.
12. Reserve smiles for breezes (not freezes).
13. Drop stitches on eaves and platforms.
14. Erase standing guidelines. Escort unexpected hemlines.
15. Count and tally glitches. Retire and retrain traditional (st)itches.
16. Stretch sashes. (S)wear wisely.
17. Dissect dialogue. Invest in foil-proof fabrics.
18. Tool wool and store women's wisdom.

Tours, Attractions, and Must-Visit Landmarks: People to Greet

Deeds, Not Words

—Emmeline Pankhurst

for women named _____

disruption

both noun
and verb. a state
of multiple tenses
and minds

an act, a word
at times articulated
often unsaid

a movement, a march
a wave of multiple degrees
and flavors of force

not all acts make headlines
not all headlines are facts

women named Mary and Maude
and Ida and Ada

threaded needles thru thistles
to pave new abodes

abundance both noun and verb
nouns and verbs in abundant form

women named Eve and April
and Susan and Syd

saw more
for future generations
than the times let on

never did they ever allow a lexicon
inked in dictionaries, dated and dotted
to dictate form

of speech and manners
of manners of address

they dressed instead
to disrupt. in, of, and
with opulence

Movement #19 (with a Chorus Named Disruption)

A red robin pecks at cobblestone. A mourning dove sings songs of sorrow. Handwritten signs atop storefronts flutter. Neither the waltz nor the tango at home on the radio. Cold winds cut as opinions (s)pool. Compass dials spin in neighborhoods with sharp corners. OPEN. CLOSED. Woolworths and its garden center are now a bank branch decorated with artificial trees and a name I cannot remember. The tailor converted to a Trader Joe's. Of dense aisles and limited miles. Familiar packaging blends with floral bouquets wrapped around samples and shoulders. Bite-sized tastings and thought free for the taking. (S)HOT.

Bartering is baked into currency and local election turnouts. The mall is now a graveyard. The movie theatre a maze of cubicles. The 24-hour diner was reimagined as an urgent care with limited hours. As new flavors of dissent come to market, the town square—fountains of soda and water—are capped then closed. ONE-WAY TRAFFIC. GRIDLOCK. NO TURNS ON RED. The spider with its eight legs wonders what to make of new webs.

Needles are discarded on streets. Rusted spickets spiral in tunnels that echo. HELLO. NO. NO. Artificial intelligence boils (foils) novelty. Antiquity unrecognized. Output a reflection of input. Binary code formulaic. The mockingbird haunts. To vote is not the same as to sing in a chorus. New movements needed. Each voice is an opportunity to solo. YAY. NAY. ANEW. A DAY. Cocoons court new ways of thinking. ChatGPT and AI acronyms reply. Critters conspire. To vote is a duel of butterflies and spotted lantern flies. Wings stretched. ASK WHY.

Cycles of wishes continue. Today anticipates tomorrow as local newspapers shutter. Shadows of pasts, presents, and futures pool. Children toss pennies at dawn (heads and teeth brushed, tales turned) and chase fireflies at dusk. Specks of light. Flashes of wonder. Eruption and disruption both noun and verb.

The march to Number 19 was not cheap, though the marchers were often depicted as such. I wonder what Alice Paul would say to today's favored and flavored forms of think (and drink). Cocktails on all corners. Gowns and guns with hems out of order. The need for disruption neither conflated nor inflated. Change and Susan B. Anthony dollars needed. Dependent on those, like Paul, willing to march. To think. To mix new drinks.

Who Am I?

I am Lucy Burns, born on July 28, 1879. In Brooklyn, Kings, New York, United States of America. United, a relative term. My first cry was delivered approximately twelve miles from the Atlantic Ocean. This will also be the place of my last breath. Our house was full. And fair. I am the fourth of eight children. Sister of Mary, Anna, Helen, Charles, Robert, and two more. My parents—Edward and Ann had five daughters and three sons. Mother and Father believed in education and equal opportunity for all their children. No matter. Neither could assure me, us, my sisters, equal rights outside of the home.

No

My name is Lucy. I have red hair and blue eyes. I stand five feet seven inches. I study linguistics and equal rights. I prefer freedoms to tensions. I refuse to comply. I am teacher and trainer. All feelings ripe. I see no reason why the vote for women should be denied. I wear dresses, corsets, and pants. I take a stance. I fancy bloomers. Envision a world where all women can dance. I favor freedoms to boiled potatoes and fried chicken. I have friends. Alice. Emmeline, Christabel, and Sylvia. The tiny mice that share my cell. The owl that watches the guards in boots. And, also, many foes.

Not right

I'm Lucy. I believe in equal rights. I hold no vote. Neither myself nor my sisters have a say. We're of the census yet censured. No one knows our names. There is no shame, we believe, in equality. Our bodies are the same. Our bodies our different. We think. We know. We desire. More. We insist on a right to vote. To suffrage. To know. To no suffering. Watch. Watch us. We fight.

Closer

I've grown used to being watched without being named. I am that girl. The one who inspires pain, who causes trouble, who exhibits disdain. For what? I think. Rules with no regard for the women they sink. I am that girl. From the eye of a third person: Brooklyn, 1879. A place of cobblestone and stones to turn. A small child born in the shadow of the night. Hair ablaze. Ready to fight. Birthed to parents who prioritized education. Their girls would plan and plant new paths. Origins known. Futures yet grown. I am that girl.

Tonight

The human body is as much machine as sky. Spirit and soul require sustenance. All flames depend on coal. I am cold. I am tired. I am hungry. I am incarcerated. I've done no harm. I've gained no happiness. My intentions are acts of untimely, though peaceful, resistance. The time I've spent in prison is time denied. My work. My life. A quest. For equal rights. Of sisters on both sides of the Atlantic. I shall not stop. I need to rest. Surely the treatment couldn't get any worse. I am cold. I am tired. I am hungry. I will refuse all sustenance. There is only one offering. That of equal rights. I'd like a bowl of soup. I toss their soup aside. I am that girl. I drop my pen. I do not sleep. I wait. I anticipate. More men.

Josephine Butler / To Lift the "Fallen Women"

to say that a woman named Josephine
built structures, baked legislation, and
dismantled acts that placed women
in locked down habitations

    wouldn't say enough

to aptly describe her work
of twisted knuckles
and unleashed buckles
for the "fallen women"

she hammered. she nailed.
she negotiated deals. she
constructed trails

of open homes and hostels
legislation to overturn coverture
and no ownership domiciles

she built frames and made space
for "fallen women" to be their
own legal entity

    themselves, enough

with property and rights
and unlocked limbs

to acknowledge a woman
named Josephine refused
to accept _____ or _____

    doesn't say enough

a woman named Josephine
had seen enough.

A Woman Named Josephine

A woman named Josephine had seen enough. she knew better than to accept the day's daily news *(subservience de jure)*. instead, she cast notions of second-class status aside and inked, blinked, and opened rooms. with drapes of lace and safety of place, women slept. free from the subordination of existing law. on mattresses stuffed of freedom. women (s)wept. vocabulary heavy of liberty. women earned rest (and trust). in peace. of place. and gained strength. to test (and stretch). to fight. to theorize. against corseted waists, locked gates, and dictated space.

i wonder what she, Josephine, might say, today, of the skies, the present states of affairs, and decisions likes *Roe v. Wade, Obergefell v. Hodges,* and *Dobbs v. Jackson Women's Health Organization.* i think, she'd blink. ponder what next to do. then act. perhaps she'd ink haiku.

mourning dove coos code
on phone wires
not all flocks are ~~loyal~~ legal

men in (pur)suits (t)read
as property transfers
bleed—signs of the times

baby birds flap wings
as judges in bow ties (s)weep
flocks (of ~~fallen~~ women) roar

the Court
a popular institution
of structural foundations flawed

coverture's howls echo
limbs unlock laces
and renewed paces

women in bloomers
pin loyalties on chicken wire
then march to court (no escort needed)

a woman named Josephine thinks, acts, speaks

overheard in Parliament

women's suffrage
equal parts (f)right
and (b)light

to think,
that eggs and legs
could stir such a stink

women in black boots
march through red and yellow leaves

      —Movement #19

Getting Around

I think [the bicycle] has done more
to emancipate women than any one thing in the world.
I rejoice every time I see a woman ride by on a bike.

—Susan B. Anthony

She's Got Legs

legs that walk miles with no nylons
up, down, cross town—bloomers
on boulevards

baked and basked, rationed and stitched,
threaded and tasked. in patterns of plaid
and layers of cotton, wool, and linen

    she's got legs

legs that talk to unfamiliar
audiences. legs that refuse to balk.
legs that give the boot to corsets
and wide-rimmed skirts.

legs that trash awkward styles and
rewrite news bytes. swap hoops
for sturdy swatches sketched of ink.

legs that crush resistance, marches,
and out-of-tune wedding bells.

legs in full bloom—petals and
patterns punctuated of steps on stairs
and dismissals of airs.

legs in step—eager to navigate
sharp l(edges). skilled in fresh
cuts and stitched fabrics.

finely tooled (no instructions needed)
steeped of attitude in full bloom

    she's got legs

The Egret

auto corrected
in colonies (of unspoken
words, metaphors,
and unused verbs)

nearby shores,
of calm palms
and familiar psalms—

once   provoked,   it   blooms

A Collection of Micro-Reflections
/ on the Women Who Marched

to march
in March
and not say
I do

March,
a month of cautions,
clichés, and calendar
clay. In and of lions.
Lambs touted in
upcoming horizons.
Men anticipate.
Women contemplate.
  No, but—
  Yes, and—
A(wait)
M(arch)
Per(colate)
Ampersands proliferate.

to discard
purses
and pursed
lips
to wash
hands of harsh
arses
and press
anew
  as we wish

An Abecedarian Demanding Attention
/ and No Further Mention of Success

Abigail was a popular baby name in 1834,
        the year Abigail Jane Scott Duniway was
born. Britannica.com—a pop-up
        for the reference claims,
        "find the answers, trust the facts"—
        states that she's remembered
"chiefly" for her ultimately successful pursuit
        of reform. While the text notes that
"Despite her efforts, Duniway's main goal,
  equal suffrage for women in Oregon,
        eluded her, her efforts
        nonetheless bore
fruit elsewhere" and I think -
gee-whiz. *Initial response edited.*
        due emphasis denied.
        the bar unjustly high.
        a woman named Abigail
        Jane Scott Duniway
        of Oregon, not
her state of origin. Born in
Illinois. Her subject being
        a woman's right to vote.
        Duniway
        did things her way—
Justice sought and seized
        one step at a time.
        I wonder who
        writes the pieces
        that proclaim to recognize
        a life. Puzzles on parade.
        There's no such thing
        as paradise. With
        emphasis on output,
        rather than input.

Karma created in tales
      of classrooms and books.
      of prairie crossings
      and legal
limitations overturned. Duniway was
      ultimately
      the first woman
      to register to vote
      in the state of Oregon.
      and an example
      of what a life well-lived means
means to be remembered
      someone
      with a common
      name who did uncommon things
      when every step is a piece
      of a complex puzzle
not necessarily a win in an
overt offering. But an owner of
Notions and millineries.
Of tales and stories. Of
published works—including
      the first novel
      written in the Pacific Northwest.
      The New Northwest. Speaking tours.
      Poetry collections. The Oregon
      Equal Suffrage Association. The
      Pacific Empire. So. Much. More.
Quiet work of words at play
Rarely do the reference books
      prioritize
      tones and tunes
      of remarkable times
Sigh. the history of suffrage and
success measured
      in utterly peculiar ways
      Why can't Britannica remember

Abigail and others
for work done, not intermediary
targets and teasers denied.
Probably for the same reason that International
Women's Day remains an annual event and
Men as Champions for Women Awards
remains a recurring theme
rather than a daily document
Underdogs constantly under an umbrella
Verified wins waxed, watered, and waned
"What's a life, anyway"? Charlotte asked Wilbur
Amidst webs both tangled and thundered
"We're born, we live a little, we die"
Touché. We pine for
Xtra time, always more. To realize
years (75 and counting—more)
of yearning stitched
of raspberry-scented fingers
and blueberry-flavored wishes
With success measured
Most
Best
Always
In the
Zigzags—not the destination

Travel Costs

The total cost of the [Suffrage Parade of 1913] was $14,906.08, a princely sum in 1913, when the average annual wage was $621.

I Followed Him

after hours pacing
the 3-dimensional
spaces between

        (s)he and I
        truth and lie
        asymmetrical radii

        points
        of latitude and longitude
        increasing

she

took twelve paces
South, then East,
then North
then West

drafted a trapezoid
where a square
once sat

she

dropped a ring
on the counter

circumference, diameter
radii (times two) denied

not all sides are
equivalent

not all angles are
acute

some cases obtuse / not
yet
shut

      stretched
      starched
      stitched
      crossed
      knotted

patterns
and patches

cast fishhooks
and caught players

hand-sewn in layers
of lace and gingham
on doors and windows

she minded the children
tended the chickens
adopted bloomers

played games
of hide

      and seek
      then marched

to court
to vote
to speak

*a woman named ___ (*St. Louis Post-Dispatch,* October 20, 1920)

To Quote a Quilt

- hems tucked (and stuck)
- backsides primed (a grind)
- waists waiting (and weighting)
- stitches (and itches) soaked in calamine
- needles in motion (craving lotion)
- exorbitant costs tallied (rules rallied)
- unequal sides damning (inequities glaring)

—the quill pen

The Suffragist

The Suffragist published political drawings. A woman named
Nina Allender the cartoonist. Elegant and articulate, the Allender
Girl was the first to move. Hands on hips. Mountains of paper.
Moments to pause. Both ink and needles drew nods and notice.
Toils and souls. In print and on unpaved soil—original versions
of the modern woman. *The Suffragist*—both a noun and a verb. of
origins and unplanned Panels

Out-of-style

> wood paneling
> and performative speaking
> clip bits and bytes of speech
> women tout *Tide*
> brand in polyester
> pants

In-style

> original tiling
> and styling—no
> gel, all tells
>
> brushed locks
> and plot twists—
> marches thru
> marshes, women
> in board seats

The Cost of a Dress (Amelia Jenks Bloomer)

There was a time

when I believed the price

of fashion was a simple

case of arithmetic. Calculations

that even I, despite my

limited mathematics education,

could compute with ease.

Add, subtract, divide.

Reams of fabric

Thread

Spools

Patterns

Scissors

Needle

Time

Combine a gown with a short skirt,

Cut and measure to the upper shin,

With a pair of long, luxurious

Poofy pants. Divine!

Add a bishop (mate!)

Or pagoda sleeve (the steps not

Unlike a match of chess, I believe) along with

A blouse for required modesty.

Gather the bloomer into a cuff,

Hook atop the ankle

(delicate!),

Nearly done!

Or not.

Who knew emotions would multiply.

Now, I know better

Even As Elizabeth

(Cady Stanton)

has framed the challenge,

Her own cousin my first

Introduction to the stylish pattern,

she's privately confessed,

"Had I counted

the cost of the short dress,

I would never have put it on."

Staying Safe: Tips and Reminders

The best protection a woman can have . . . is courage.

—Elizabeth Cady Stanton

Women at a Crossroads: 20 (plus) Ways to Disrupt a Timeline

1. To vote :: an exercise in disruption
2. when reasons :: to march are many
3. and identity :: crosses lines
4. Marked and monitored :: by souls
5. demanding spots :: named mine
6. Soles stretched of leather :: boots tied and knotted
7. Primed to trace pathways :: performed and paraded
8. Grace :: on full display
9. As language lingers :: on handwritten signs
10. Habits haunt hallways :: and hallmarks of timelines
11. Feedings :: in nostrils
12. Beatings :: on buttocks
13. The price :: paid by some
14. The prize :: lost for none
15. To vote :: is it more noun or verb
16. To march :: to generate speech in new forms
17. Of gowns and grains :: by the pound
18. Of witch hunts :: and hounds
19. Ultimate disruptions :: converted for all time
20. from past :: to present and future forms

women named _____ and _____.
also _____, marched in
irregular form. on asphalt,
in linen, of (p)lace and thyme.

in high-heels and high-
tide. of all forms of speech.
a statement of movements
and moments turned minutes
for all time (and timelines)

/ each mark / march
a stitch

/ of disruption
in dress / addressed

some say she doth _____too much :: on forms (and performances) of speech

in june 2022, on the heels of injustice and feet (bare and bruised) from the supreme court, women held signs with scripts of rights and fights— *my body my rights / abort the court / we're not ovary-acting*—over tanks. words of weariness (unchanged) and war (for change) brushed shoulders with humidity and visibility. a media blitz / tempers on the fritz. police along perimeters. all corners crafted. all orders drafted. *marcha*. rubber soles kissed asphalt. cries of *marcha*-kissed lips. in past, present, and future tense. of grammar and gripes both (im)proper and (ir)regular. *"the lady doth protest too much, methinks"* wrote shakespeare. blends of nouns, verbs, and adjectives. hamlet performed on stages / in texts / along gravel roads. *marcha*. through histories both hot and haunting. from the 1789 march on versailles to the suffrage parade of 1913. handwritten signs with scripts of rights and fights—*mr. president / how long must women wait for liberty*—alongside tanks. strikes for equality in 1970 *(equal positions with equal pay)* and marches for peace in 1976. *marcha*. of inauguration protests *(judge women as people not as wives)* and pro-choice marches (my mind, my body, my freedom). of events large—the women's march in 2017. and small—daily duos of time and space. crowds chant—*marcha*. rubber soles kiss asphalt. language lingers in layers. lyrics and loops of longing (and belonging). she speaks truths. vérité.

protest and march bear similarities across language. etymologies and roots blend. truths vary.

istina. pravda. sandhed. waarheid. vero. tõde. totuus. vérité.

at the foot of a future baked (staked and flaked) of fear, i type vérité into a cell. autocorrect converts my attempt at truth to bernie. not quite. next bertie. no. finally birth. tech, time, and twisted testimonies play cruel tricks. of nouns, verbs, and adjectives. time ticks. cells both technological and molecular work assumptions on lands no longer (of the) free. three backspace erasures (and even more judicial back steps) to move one step forward. and (re)write vérité.

in july 2022, americans gather to celebrate the birth of a nation /
darkness again shades gingham blankets. skies lit of storm clouds rain
nouns, verbs, and adjectives of unfathomable propositions. patriotism
a pale shadow. no longer a form of speech. *"the lady doth protest too
much, methinks"* wrote shakespeare. hamlet performed on stages
/ in texts / along gravel roads. cherry pie bleeds on soles and souls.
marcha yells a woman after telling her mother she loves her. one last
time. *marcha* yells a mother after grabbing the arm of an orphaned
child. alone. parades of protests and individual truths. handwritten
signs with scripts of rights and fights.

vérité—

real patriots / keep cool

a kiss

—is not a contract

to ask freedom / for women

is not a crime

—can makeup cover

the wounds / of our oppression

/ don't cry

    —resist / marcha

timelines both chronological
and cryptic collude. attire changes
—corsets unlaced / attitudes
persist—whalebone both
flexible and a strong maneuver.
/ those that conspire

shall not tire / a woman's
place / remains in the resistance
/ justice (on parade) cannot wait.
all reigns trained. targets
in plain sight / of gender
roles and rubber soles.
—amidst atmospheric souls.
planets revolve around a singular
sun / of fire and fuel / most all
moons in the solar system / point
faces (and fingers) at planets
bare / both moons and sun
of potions and patterns—parades
/ alignments of prepositions
and propositions / truths—*vérité*

to Pa·rade
/pə' rād/

to March
/märCH/

to Protest
/ prō,test /

in / of / on
               streets
each cell a truth
in / of / on
protest. parade.
marcha. vérité.
each cell a form

of speech
               adjectives
               verbs
               nouns

of past
and future tenses

one of the trillions
      nerves
      muscles
      connective tissue

tightly attached.
in / of / on
communication hubs.
in bold / oversized font
of wrapped text
and liquid ink
quick dry / quick wit
truths rain (to reign).

       vérité

12 (plus) reasons to march (in protest)

1. Past and future tenses predict more than pretenses.
2. Time marches. Attitudes persist. Both twist.
3. Walls are made by more than muscles. Muscles connect more than tissue.
4. Communication bubbles when (em)broiled.
5. Truths are individually verified (and verifiable).
6. Nouns, verbs, and adjectives blend (and brush) shoulders.
7. Displays of emotion cross boundaries (and forms of speech).
8. Public processions promote ponderings (and sometimes concessions).
9. Prepositions often form propositions.
10. Public squares are rarely formed of equal sides.
11. March and charm share the same letters. Syllables strung in air float.
12. Women possess (more than) charm and lead (more than) marches.
13. *Some say she doth _____ too much.*

As a Child

As a child, our household was in a constant state of suspension.
No one held any breath, but we all knew either news or objects
might drop at any time and without any notice.

My siblings and I would stay occupied with books and blocks. Beets
and Boots. Not in that order. Mostly in perpetual states of disorder.

I was forced to negotiate for everything.

Chores like laundry and meal prep. Who got the last roll at
dinner? Who was first to their preferred section in the day's
newspaper?

I'd never let my brothers one up me.

I acquired tricks. I refined tactics.

I learned to persuade. To convince.

Rinse and repeat.

I would not accept defeat.

At the time I never realized just how helpful that practice and
those skills in training could (and would) be.

Father liked it that way. He'd say our home prepared us for a life
on the big stage.

I'd listen, then reach for *The New York Times* front page.
"Why do you care about the news," my brother would say.

"Why don't you?" I'd reply.

"You act like you expect to see your own name in there," he'd tease,
often with a huff and a sigh.

I'd nod and consume. I loved the language and the layers of meaning hidden in the headlines.

One day I read this headline in *The New York Times*.

On the 3rd of January in 1897.

The digits the reverse of my own year of birth.

"DO WOMEN HATE WOMEN?"

With sub-text that reads

"A MAN SAYS THAT THEY DO, BUT THREE WOMEN SAY NOT. It Is a Question of Temperament, Says Elizabeth Cady Stanton—Dr. Hall-Brown and Mrs. Burns Emphatic."

Why in the world would they ask a man what a woman thinks, I remember thinking, then stating, then asking.

Father liked it that way.

With friends, too. We'd debate. We'd ruminate. We'd create.

Of course, sometimes, with everyone in the room silent,

we'd whisper.

Mostly to ourselves.

Are they right?

Small voices, voices from inside.

"Stop, Lucy," I'd say to silence the doubt.
Never did I ever expect to see my own name in print.

Never did I cease seeking headlines.

On November 22, 1913, I did.

I had recently been arrested.

The headline, also *The New York Times*, read:

Lucy Burns fined $1.

With subtext that read

"Militant Proudly Pays for Chalking the White House Walk."

The journalist called me—

"The Capital's first militant suffragette"

What did I write in chalked letters?

"Votes for Women"

In large block print.

In the courthouse I was forced to promise not to repeat the offense.

I told the judge I wanted the whole thing

over with. Only I didn't explain precisely what I meant.

I insisted on having the distinction of paying my fine.

Just as I would continue to insist on the distinction

for all women of the right to vote.

until next time.

a woman named Alice: inventor of _____

the hunger strike

> practiced
> cheerful
> did not regret
> prepared
> to repeat

food
being injected
in nostrils

tied to a chair

didn't give in

[in her own words]

left the prison
in a cab

A Jiu-Jitsu Artist's Dream

the sport
originated in Japan,
then moved, as defense
mechanisms often do,
to South America

years,

calculated
in multiples
of ten times ten,
times two (more)

exponential
expressions before
women would rally,

to gather seams,
tuck hems, and stitch
a thread through time
and through which
the jumbled jiu-jitsu artists'
expertise formed a niche

rarely routine—

punches, jabs,
and jamborees

defensive
mechanisms were needed

on streets paved
of adrenaline
and alibis

corsets tied,
prepped
to rendezvous.
redo, and remain

committed
with hammers hidden
beneath exercise mats
and armor crafted of cardboard

amidst Bodyguards placed
in secret spaces
across London

a woman named Edith,
4 feet 11 inches of vision
refined, would remain
grounded, with grown
men tossed

up down right side wrong

ATTENTION!

the shoulders
of resistance strong

the suffragists trained
in jiu-jitsu stronger still,

Edith writes (of dreams denied)—

*Why We Oppose Jiu-Jitsu for Women**

after Alice Duer Miller

1. Because police already know jiu-jitsu.
2. Because men already know jiu-jitsu.
3. Because there is no logical need for women to learn jiu-jitsu if men and police already know jiu-jitsu.
4. Because self-defense is not a natural right.
5. Because violence is not a way to right a wrong.
6. Because violence is already messy. Women have enough to clean, mend, and tend.
7. Because women are not naturally inclined to tricks of slight.
8. Because training takes time and women are already burdened with so much.
9. Because jiu-jitsu is neither easy nor effortless.
10. Because the female disposition is not aligned with violence in the streets.
11. Because armor is not the same as armour.
12. Because scissors are best suited for cuts of fabric.
13. Because rubber clubs are most appropriately used to pound chicken.
14. Because locks are designed to secure the home, the women's proper place.
15. Because a hunger for equality is easily satisfied with extra helpings of biscuits and ham.
16. Because sweat is not the same as sweet.

Best Time to Visit

That vote has been costly. Prize it!

—Carrie Chapman Catt

ascensor :: together we lift

for the women suffragists who were imprisoned and tortured in
November 1917 during a Night of Terror at Occoquan Workhouse
after a peaceful picket and a demand for equal rights

ascensor. over tea and triangle
toast metal cutlery clinks. sinks
stocked and stacked. meat meets
potatoes (both boiled) and melodic
souls meet cubes of raspberry-
flavored ice (most already diced)
/ historically placed amidst handwritten
notes. women prepare. *ascensor.*

together, we lift

the start / end of strings of days
perfectly imperfect / clothed of white
fabrics amidst fears, cotton shears
among clichés, and worn rubber
soles amidst long greased
roles. wisdom and worry blend
with vanilla tea / tea leaves and steam
simmer in open fires / eyelids shaded
of cranberry crush and lashes heavy
of charcoal—fingers stained
of ink on cardboard signs. *ascensor.*

together, we lift

amidst grass stains of stones
and walking sticks, vaulted
(and salted) splashes of text simmer
/ loose threads line knickers
and plaid patches. manila envelopes
stacked / perfectly imperfect files

closed, conspiracies on silent and diaries
locked. *ascensor*.

    together, we lift

fabric-draped limbs extend
longing / elbows worn,
skin near torn—locked (and loaded)
transcripts ready. strings of syllables
dangle, inciting / fire and fury. *ascensor*.

    together, we lift

in
white houses / in white
blouses
at dawn and dusk

/ in and of straps—
groups of women. stake
claims and claim space. conduct
and conspire. pickets in peace. *ascensor*.

    together, we lift

before/during/after fights for rights
and nights of terror / in and of walls—
both literal and ordered. together,
we lift. *ascensor*—a 1917 group
of women. thirty-three in number
/ representative of infinite more.
years and souls. times and travels
multiplied. multi-dimensioned.

occoquan guards both guarded
and on demand. requests for treatment

as political prisoners denied. safety
deprived / prison superintendent william
whittaker orders guards to not guard
but to terrorize / limbs clocked—ladies
dragged, then flogged and (f)locked. *ascensor.*

together, we lift

dorothy day / a 'frail girl'
of fight and rights. subject to the
arms of prison guards / an occoquan
workhouse resident, accused and abused
—of dissidence. her arms twisted
/ her head down. struck against an iron
bench. once. again. *ascensor.*
together, we lift

mary nolan / the group
of thirty-three's elder. a subject
and subject to a sentence constructed
of prepositions and propositions
highly irregular. verbs on fire.
proper nouns at risk. adjectives
of new (and newly inspired) shame.

all members
of the national woman's party.
a group of 'silent sentinels'
spent moments—minutes
turned days / turned months—in
peaceful form and fashion. arms lifted.
fingers inked. banners
and placards stained
—seeking the right to vote. *ascensor.*

we lift, together

during a night
of terror. one of many.
on the path to persistence.
a journey of many steps, stops, then starts.
a journey behind and beside (in and of) daily walls.
a journey of cinder blocks. and cells with no clocks.
heavy of propositions and prepositions. *ascensor*. together, we lift.

with a destination both moving and of a movement / never beyond
the horizon. of dusk and dawn. lids, lashes and breasts heavy.
souls on soiled floors. hands on metal bars. fingers tug
on desire / at worms. arms raised. bodies rise.
amidst steps, stops, and stones. *ascensor*.

together we lift

lucy burns / spent the night standing
hands shackled and attached to a cell's
ceiling. threatened with straitjackets
and buckle gags. dorothy day / slammed
against an iron bench. once. twice.

day turns to night / day lies unconscious
and alice cosu / eyes trace and track assaults
/ her own heart attacks. delayed care and diminished
attention. food caked of worms. water dark. bedding
soiled. feedings forced alongside transfers. two.
twelve. twenty. numbers rise
to a count of thirty-three. *ascensor*.

together, we lift

moments turn months. invitations
for coffee and complacency (with a side
of cream) refused. platitudes and patriarchy

resisted. affronts of / on patriotism amidst
war-time peculiarities withstood.
ascensor. together, we lift. women
initially arrested and released
for traffic obstructions. consume risks
and return amidst realities and recognition
of prison. silent sentinels picket
and parade. costumes carefree and carefully
constructed. fog greets the horizon
gravel nods to the rubber tires
all souls tired. spirits do not tire. *ascensor.*

together, we lift.

11 (times 3) reasons to *ascensor*
1. Terror both trains and builds testimony
2. Realities rarely conspire amidst recognition
3. Silence often speaks louder than speech
4. In small pockets of air, souls conspire
5. Paths to persist are rarely linear
6. Buckles both gap and gag
7. Straitjackets rarely suit
8. Dawn follows night (including nights of terror)
9. Ink both stains and strains
10. Obstructions are multidimensional
11. Together, we lift

Judgment Day

I sat. I sat and I listened. I listened to him speak.

From a lecture. Inches from my chained feet.

I wish I had my pencil. To note his choice of speech.

He repeats. Proper nouns. Lucy. Lucy. Lucy Burns.

Queries and questions. *Who. What. Where. When. Why.*

So many contradictions. I refuse to comply.

I wish I had my pencil. To note his choice of speech.

And his frustration. Growing like my protest.

Two can play that game.

I do not think he would have liked what I wished to do.

I wish I had my pencil. To capture what I see.

> An unkempt white mustache.
> Shadows of yesterday's lunch.
> Shades of brown, blue, and gray.
> Undersized legs, clothed and draped.
> Oversized eyes, green, assessing my fate.

The crumbs dance, a form of tag, I think, as his syllables string.

The bifocals on his nose quiver.
Hypocrisy in 3-D.

I sigh.

Excuse me, he inquires.

I refuse to meet his eye.

His plumped lips read my rights

from a podium six feet high—

Balanced scales of justice denied.

I reflect. The ache in my chest still strong.

Their fingers press.

This is what I suspect. What I recollect.

Of what the judge prepped. What he planned to say.

There's more there. More than meets the eye.

His dual nature (and the nature of Judgment Day) cannot be denied.

I saw him. I heard him. Bifocals and earpieces in 2-D.

———

Overheard In the Judge's Chambers (Pre-Game Prep)

"Young lady. You know I have your best interest at heart,"

I write. As I practice my speech. She's tiring. I don't have the
energy for her escapades.

"Young lady. You know what I shall say. This is not your first day of
reckoning."

I've said it all before. She cares not. Her focus, the work of a fool.

"Ms. Burns. You stand before the court. Again. On a charge of disorderly conduct."

I shall be brief. She's caused enough grief.

I scratch initial sentiments. Dip my pen in fresh ink. Collect a new leaf.

I shall be brief.

"Ms. Burns," I say.

"Do you understand the charges of which I speak?"

She'll nod, I suspect.

Fiery red hair. Blue eyes. A waste.

She'd make a fine wife if only she weren't so easily despised. So easy to rise.

I'll wait.

Let the crowds anticipate my next move. My charge. As the head of the court.

Once all eyes return, I'll continue to speak.

The irony. To think that she believes she could make me blink.

I've paid my dues in time and dress.
I've studied legal texts.
I've sat for multiple tests.
I've voted for comrades.

Can she claim all of that?

Ms. Burn's achievements, so small in comparison to mine.

Who, I'd like to know, does she think she is?

"Ms. Burns, please rise," I'll say in a voice so nice.

"Do you understand the charges and the penalty that will suffice?"

She will not answer. That, I know. I shall not let her.

She'll do as she's told.

A Woman Named Arabella Mansfield
/ and a Series of Questions I'd Like to Ask

In 1869, a 23-year-old woman named Arabella Babb Mansfield took it upon herself to challenge gendered language not by force, not to seek fame, but to play a fair game. She sat for an exam crafted for a man-driven nation. Her rebuke to the proposition (no prepositions needed) that only men are fit to serve as solicitors amidst a country of rations was, in the words of her examiners, "the very best". Her inspired performance demanded new proclamations.

While the exam might have remained concealed, and though Mansfield's pen might never have scratched judicial chambers, she ruled, has ruled, and has inspired infinite rulings (of both prepositions and propositions) for a less gendered set of legal tools and constructions. Mansfield was the first female attorney but, of course, not the last. A beacon, a barometer, an A+ barrister. A blend of curiosity and veracity. Tenacity and acuity. Dressed of prefixes and accolades undenied. Arabella Mansfield knew not only the bar's ABCs but also how to weave strings of letters turned syllables into a series of never-before "can dos"—from A through Z. An educator who sought to pass on, not over, those who'd walk beside her, Arabella Mansfield crafted, compelled, and transformed the world.

What a gift it would be to know more of Mansfield's pioneering escapades. Of formative and summative perspectives. If only we could sit, perhaps over tea, and engage in conversation grounded in legal philosophy. There are infinite questions I'd like to ask. Mostly, to recap—the test, the rest, the history, and all *That*. I wonder.

What might Mansfield say about *That*? Not the legalities or the multiple-choice frivolities. True/False binaries just as wrong *Then* as *Now*. But at the intersection of Arabella, the woman, and the law, on trial. On the ballot and ballad of her writing. On the sentiments and senses of her life. I'd really like that.

I'd ask:

1. Was sitting for the bar more (or less) decision than destiny?
2. Was fighting the ruling more (or less) conviction than opposition?
3. Did you ever question if you would pass?
4. Which was the question that should have been rewritten?
5. Which response provided the most satisfaction?
6. Which question prompted the greatest frustration?
7. How would you define "to raise the bar"?
8. Which question inappropriately used a woman as the defendant?
9. Which question inappropriately used a male as the plaintiff?
10. Which question was first? Which question was last?
11. Was there a question that made you smile?
12. Was there a question with an excessive number of adverbs (or adversaries)?
13. Was there a question with only inappropriate answers?
14. Was there a question that should never have been asked?
15. Was the exam more frivolity or formula? Was the proctor kind?
16. What are your thoughts on the Mansfield Rule? Do you approve of the phrasing?
17. Did you hear the scratch of the men's pencils? The tap of their feet?
18. Did the room have a scent? A sense of anticipation?
19. How did you dress? How were you addressed?
20. Was the room inviting? Were the stares piercing?
21. Was there a question about eligibility to serve?
22. Did you bring your own pencil, fully sharpened?
23. What was your breakfast of champions? What is the flavor of a rebuke?
24. From what point of view did you offer your response? Was it a good time?

Mostly I'd listen
/ and give thanks

for a series of firsts
/ not lasts

—across time

women named bitch

i grew up on tv dinners—salisbury steak and mashed potatoes,
roast turkey and stuffing, always with a side of frozen green beans.
on days i'd been naughty there'd be no dessert. on days i'd been nice,
a slice of sara lee all-butter pound cake. thawed to room temperature.
the freezer both a keeper and a counter. rarely did the table
bare anything fresh. all mouths monitored.

soap—usually ivory sometimes dove,
was always on the menu. all mouths
in a perpetual state of readiness. conversation
carefully waxed and washed while elders
would toss curse words like salad.
some in excess. some in exile. contradictions
hidden in plain sight.

for years i'd been told that bitches were canines
and that only dogs begged—food the price
to pay for freedom. *where's freedom*, i'd ask,
eyes and mouth open. then be told to shut up
and shut down. flies in a perpetual state
of fluctuating readiness.

i grew up thinking sons of bitches were insults
meant for men of stature. the kind that whistled
when i walked to and from the public elementary.
and the kind that whacked my bottom
when i wavered. mathematics
never my strength. rulers everywhere.

i did not understand that all terms are borrowed.
and that not all that is borrowed is meant to be worn.
and that not all that is sworn is meant to be secret.

and that everybody
doesn't like something

and that language surges like adrenaline
tossed shotgun
and that dirty laundry airs and dries
even if bloomers and knickers prompt rumors and snickers

/ extra peanuts

until i stumbled
on magick in motion
/ and learned

that a woman named bitch
tied brown lug-soled shoes
with charcoal laces
and secured heavy cotton
lace-ups with corsets and nylon hose

and kissed her children on the forehead,
all locks freshly washed of castile
soap and canthrox shampoo

and packed sandwiches
of sardines, olives, and eggs
in her tote

     —all hard boiled
       tempers, too

and rode by horse,
carriage, and courage
to a march on 5th

     and ten months later
     she cast her first vote

and that not only sara lee
is portion controlled
and that insults are as cheap
as day-old bread

and that private and public
spheres

potions	politics
potlucks	notions
waists	weights
waits	waste

women (named bitch)

have bounds,
many with prohibitions
and extra rounds
and that i don't need
to be monitored or liked
and that i too can persist

amidst scoldings for backwash
in tropicana lemonade,

awash in backlash for bitching
about cheerleaders on parade

and that shotguns and wedding plans
and downtown hunts

for something new (uptown),
something borrowed (barely),
something blue (maybe)

are as much backlash as whiplash

as i learned about backlash
and bitches—not sons
of anyone, but daughters

turns out that all terms are borrowed
and not all that is borrowed is meant to be worn
and not all that is sworn is meant to be secret
and not everyone needs to be liked

behavior in perpetual states
of portion control.
all plates patrolled.

and i learned
sara lee (whom nobody doesn't like)
nor its server has no relation

to—
sara bard field
sara andrews spencer
sarah jane baines
sarah benett

though just as delicious (while deemed pernicious)

heavy hitters
smooth as butter
appropriately bitter

eager to pitch a fork / not in a cut of salisbury
but a plate (and state) of higher stakes

/ of magick and motions

amongst women named bitch

of hands and handiwork :: a woman named _____

each summer, the local strip mall ran a sale. *christmas in july*
beckoned in thick, expo marker block print on laminated card
stock. births and birthdays marked. mr softee trucks (chocolate
and vanilla) and philadelphia water ice carts (cherry, lemon, and
blueberry) would idle alongside giant air men (smiles always
on). arms groped / common tropes on perpetual display. most
proprietors on wheels. some on stilts. peddling and handiwork often
a matter of perspective. the small stores (mostly mom and pops,
some staffed by tots) put out (then pushed) racks full of fabrics.
plaids and tartans. cowboy hats and high-end wool slacks. some
stitched by hand and hard work. others by automated handiwork.
items deeply discounted. potential sales marked. the sidewalk would
fill early. before the sun hit its strongest mark. everyone eager for
three-for-ten-dollar cotton tees, tie-dye scarves, and half-price denim.
cuffs hemmed, seams tucked. i'd spend my time sorting and shuffling
through cardboard boxes tucked just beneath the long skirts / sized x
small to xx large. ample fabric to conceal ankles and oglers.

i believed the shopkeeper stocked the box / a special lot for space-
saving purposes / perhaps to save face. judgment paraded in plain
sight. i also believed in santa claus. and tooth fairies. and that the
box bode not only threads, but tidings. the box held items no longer
favored for public consumption. mismatched socks. faded lots.
bleach spots. specks and stains. crisscrossed seams. last season's
winning teams. neither knock-offs nor cast-offs. mostly one-
offs. stocked, stacked, and stored for properly threaded time and
temperaments. one summer, a new set of racks was added / front
and center / to the traditional lot-sized celebration. rows of purple,
white. and green. hues both hangry and turn of key. pre-sorted / not
by size or season. but color. shirts and shirtwaists. shawls and covers
for stalls. all stitched by hand. strings of letters—*not for sale*—
handwritten in cursive print on the side of cardboard signs.

the shop's owner was a woman whose name (and name tag)
changed with the day and the seasons. each july, she was leonora.

hand-written in large block font. she'd sew most of her own merchandise. mostly while the locals would whisper. *pettiness on parade,* she'd say. i chose to linger—toil with the fabric. finger seams. read labels like library books. tee's with black and white images of 1915 parades. nyc / down 5th. washington dc / along pennsylvania. protests and protests. ironed and threaded. all corners clipped and lycra stretched. all cotton prepped and limits stitched.

did you make these? i'd ask

in the USA, the woman would snap / then smile

make a stitch, she'd gesture / then teach me

how not to follow patterns, but to thread new knots. all steps clocked. all shirts and stitches stocked—of time and tradition. she'd wonder out loud while she worked. i'd listen. like a woman named leonora. she sought to agitate the locals. she'd sit in a hard-back chair to the right of the racks. shoulders locked. and sew. deliver words like daily stitches. her needle and thread traced time to november 1909. to mark not christmas in july. the new york shirtwaist strike of 1909. through march 1910. an uprising of 20,000 knots. by then i had learned there was no such thing as santa claus. neither fairies nor fair weather. all claws hidden in plain sight. most knots manmade (and made of man). clauses inked of cotton fibers. all seams sealed. all soles squared. then clocked.

her fingers
would move in rapid
motion. each of three bones,
all named
according to the relationship
/ both proximal and technical
to the palm of her hand.
all palms

tellers of futures and fortunes.
all paths
clocked and clacked. shirts
and seconds stitched
all seams
of sermons.

her thumb
alone with no middle
/ phalange
and the persistent
push and pull
alone amidst fabrics
of varying
weights and tension

each shirt	of a trillion
stitches	each stitch
a cell	a building
block	of knots

of life, liberty,
and the pursuit

of _____

in an america

a base	not basic
a structure	not structured
nutrient serving	not notorious
an uprising	not upright

in an america

of ____ / not to be consumed
composed of membranes

/ nor confused
of mud and mocha-flavored memories—

                baste / running
                catch / blanket
                back / whip
                slip / ladder
                a thread of
                a trillion

        knots /
        and cotton tees

in an america

our dna. our rna. our rights. shirts on racks.
deeply discounted. each stitch a cell.
/ each thread a t(r)ack. stocked and stacked.
smocks of purple, white, and green on backs.
(not) for sale. of knots and needles. at the local
strip mall. threaded / at the six-month mark.

12 (plus) ways to thread (move) a needle :: it's christmas in july
1. Trade corsets for cottons (and needlers for knowledge)
2. Harness handiwork and hand-me-downs
3. Gather garments and gatherings
4. Layer fabric (and labor)
5. Agitate aggressors. Box confessors
6. Knead knots (and knotted labels)
7. Organize buttons and bandwidth
8. Curate collars and corners. Thread strands of syllables
9. Examine all sales and tales. Question all claws and clauses (claus, too)
10. Peddle serious sales. Maintain handiwork in perpetual perspective
11. Shirk standard shirts and sermons (standards, too)
12. Strip racks (trace new tracks)

Food, Table Games,
and After-Dinner Drinks

We do as much, we eat as much, we want as much.

—Sojourner Truth

To Toast

1. Another word for win(e)
2. The first name of a suffragist
3. A flavor of juice
4. Something sweet. Noun. Plural.
5. Something valued. Noun. Plural.
6. Another word for determination
7. The scent of determination
8. Another word for freedom

Alice Paul raised a glass of grape juice when the 19th Amendment was ratified. Her eyes were bright. Her dress was white. There were neither concerns nor remorse for the possibility of a stain or a lack of sustenance surmised. The year was 1920 and Prohibition came with a hefty price (and penalties). The 18th Amendment forbid the manufacturing, transportation, and sale—in combinations or permutation, in and of order—of alcohol on U.S. grounds. The women had marched then wove paths and patterns for over seventy years. As souls in rubber soles cemented change, the Constitution gained new ruffles. Fluffed and frocked. Tufted and clocked. The right to vote sweeter than any chocolate-dusted truffle. Women led movements for both temperance and suffrage. In saloons with heirs neither alto nor soprano. Lips tangoed with liquor. Work waltzed with wonder. Suffragists wanted for __ 1 __ then waited, never faltered. Disruption on all corners. Women named Annie, Charlotte, Hazel, and __ 2 __ stirred movements and avoided gut punches. They mixed new flavors and many more cosmopolitan threads. Teams sewed mixes and knitted tea party knickers. Amidst winks. By candle wicks. Surrounded by xylophone sticks. Equal pay a fight for a new day. Public spheres a ring in which to play. The home both hot and cold. A blend of hostesses and cocktail composites. As coalitions merged in odd and untold quarters, grape stains soaked bread. Disruption tangoed with hope. Curious blends of societal __ 3 __ juices brewed. Wide-brim grins spread. Marches forward of, for, and by women. Of mixing and making. Disruption and dancing. The suffragists would toast. Of __ 4 __, For __ 5 __, In __ 6 __, Amidst air heavy of __ 7 __, To __ 8 __, To disruption.

10 (Plus) Ways to Fuel and Feed a Hunger

1 :: The march was a mix of deliberate planning and spontaneous collaboration. Protesters from all corners. A fiery mix of ingredients. Seamstresses and secretaries. Teachers and time stampers. Homemakers in sneakers. Solidarity in seams. Threaded of white cotton and blue-collar themes.

2 :: The cart arrived before dawn. A combination of engine meets fire. Business dependent upon crossed wires and crosshairs. Of intersections and independent pursuits. Aware of the potential for spontaneous reactions and reactors of multiple means. Ridiculous questions of soldiers and sailors. The *Times* not alone in querying sensibilities.

3 :: The hot dog cart mobile thanks to wheels that turn on grease. Its owner well-aware of the power of metal that squeaks. He had a permit to please. And a hat to tip. Milk roll blankets. Sauerkraut on top. Bellies rumble. His cart a means.

4 :: Red-hot dachshund sausages not the only rage. A source of sustenance and solidarity. Amidst juxtapositions of many shades. Women with babies in streets. Police with paddles taking sides. Boots on asphalt. Parades of pride. Permission comes at a price. Five-cent dogs. All pennies pinched. All dollars (and dolls) counted.

5 :: He set the cart on concrete. A plot at a corner off 5th. Then watched those seeking to conquer what's right. Carefully choreographed chaos amidst always odd coordinates. All tempers moderated.

6 :: The women gathered in protest. Marched for their right to vote. He was a quiet chap. Found his voice in the power not to protest but to provide nourishment without notice. He'd boil premium sausage links and watch arms link. Food both a fuel and a fire for desire. Hot dogs in water. All tempers on boil. Offered extra condiments amidst strength in cooperation.

7 :: He knew the feeling well. Understood the need and the role of sides. Boiled all wieners. Fed all tempers. Paired dogs with spicy mustard and a splash of ketchup. Progress takes both time and proper temperament.

8 :: For him, it wasn't about the money but the mission. He'd tuck an extra roll in brown parcel bags. Then wink as marchers selected a drink. Not to quench a thirst, but to support the fight. There are many ways to fuel a hunger. To vote.

*New York's 1915 Suffrage Parade

Titles of Women Who Took to the Streets
/ a Recipe, Stewed and Sown

Equal Parts: Queen of the Mob, the Ugly London
Seamstress, and the Jiu-jitsu Suffragette.

A Pinch of the Tower Suffragette, the Flight
Teacher, and the oldest suffragist in Nassau
County

Dollops of doing across all oceans.

Stir. Strew. Repeat. Redo.

Aviators, Cartoon Creators. Self-Defense
Teachers. Parade Planners.

A blend of many spices. One goal, one
demand—diced and sliced. Prepped
and plated. A serving for all seasons.
A fight for all reasons.

Dear Alice

I wonder what you'd say,

if now
—so many years
counting, always
more
after the day
Amendment 19 was first
approved,

the Equal Rights Amendment,
proposed though not (yet) realized,

the era layered of clouds and
curiosities. Hazards and peculiarities.
Pendulums and atrocities.

If we spoke about
pockets,

hidden and clothed,
buttoned and loathed.
packed and plotted.

and what it means

      to oppose.

Alice, with your work
now
now in the public domain,

the work of the suffragist
never
never in vain.

always more
more work to be done.

     pockets to parse
     seams to sew
     threads to pluck

luck neither abundant
nor accurate

I wonder what you might say
if we talked about denim
and pocketbooks

and steps, both high-heeled
and lug-soled, forward

alongside fast fashion
trends and hot takes
with political bends

what might you say
if you knew that now
thrift shops are in vogue

in part due
due to impulses
out of control

Consumption
on all corners
contradictions
of all creators

threads and leaded
political polls
dutifully plotted

patterns emerge

a recent election
contested

weapons hidden in pockets
of gaping holes

Would you still
still oppose
pockets for women

    I'd like to know

If only we could meet
perhaps for a drink,
Oh, what a treat

Here is what I think

More reasons to (continue to) oppose pockets for women

after (and for) Alice Duer Miller

1. Because that which is concealed need not be revealed (or reviled).
2. Because one cannot deny the indiscretions that pockets might inspire.
3. Because compliance requires all hands on deck. Translucency and powder compacts are too fragile for front or back-seaming.
4. Because there's too much work left to be done. Pockets would surely distract more than they'd impact.

5. Because pockets have no utility for tasks of domesticity. And in any event, utility is neither inclusive nor exclusive to domesticity.

6. Because social media demands full transparency. Too many chicks ready to hatch.

7. Because asynchronous forms of communication expect immediacy. Women must be ready.

8. Because pockets, unlike secrets, or lockets, cannot be secured under lock and key.

9. Because pockets, like women, are prime for the picking. It's important to reveal all digits with full transparency.

10. Because women know better than to expect regular patterns (plaid, tartan, etc.) of balances and checks.

11. Because preparations for public displays and consumption must occur before leaving home.

12. Because shapes must always be molded. The flexibility of the pocket is far too unpredictable.

13. Because women already have feet. And backs. And eyes. And now, of course, a voting right. Why, in good heavens, would they have any expectation or need for more than that?

14. Because the nature of the pocket is contrary to desires for seamless transfers of power and wrinkle-free faces.

15. Because tampons and tubes of lipstick, the most likely candidates for pocket picks, are best left at home.

16. Because women can now exercise their pick in political contests. Why would they ever want to subject themselves to pocket picks while walking home?

Souvenirs

I would have girls regard themselves
not as adjectives but as nouns.

—Elizabeth Cady Stanton

How It Feels: On the Issue of Women's Suffrage

the year before,

a participant
observer
proposed

Free Press

the event
a dancehall
the lecture
a hitch

fringe
and all
public
declarations
of support

the movement

How to Be: The Husband of a Suffragette

You

on the sidewalk

go home

wash the dishes

mind the baby

indulge the guard

don't

taunt   ostracize

tag   forget

you

go   back

remember

your part

To (Be a) Witness: Found in the Clerk's Report Transport

Court is

[illegible]

a village

to Judge

under oath

in attendance

entitled

to [sum] names

DUE

Ordered

Pay

Report

A Woman Indicted

women

       being then and there

named

Hannah Chatfield

       one of several
       of the female sex

Ellen S. Baker

       one of several
       of the female sex

Nancy M. Chapman

       one of several
       of the female sex

Jane Cogswell

       one of several
       of the female sex

Rhoda DeGarmo
Susan M. Hough
Mary Hibbard
Margaret Leyden

       one of several
       of the female sex

[more ... always more]

       for illegal voting

       a true bill

How to [confuse] Incite a Citizenry: In Plain Sight

Order of Indictment
Indictment
Recognizance

(promise to the court)

[times two times four times more]
[in june of the year prior to 1874]

Did knowingly wrongfully and unlawfully vote

Be it remembered
Duly appointed

To take acknowledgments
Of bail and affidavits
To take depositions

And the jurors aforesaid

Pursuant to the provisions
Being duly, severally sworn
In the forgoing recognizance

Depose and say
He is a freeholder

[our right]

U.S. Attorney

TRUE BILL

An Abecedarian on International Women's Day

Alright, he says, after a sip
      of stale coffee, the agenda is ready,
baked and boiled of names from diverse soil
Check for canned language? a suit
      of pressed pinstripes asks,
      corporate cupcake and
      Crossword (*The New York Times* Mini) in hand
Done, the speaker smiles,
Everything Everywhere All at Once
      seized the multiverse (and airwaves) in style, we'll
fight. We'll follow. Find a way to surprise and
grab attention in ways that make
      waves and highlight our oh-so-good intentions
How about using ChatGPT
      for drafting? Good idea.
Hit me up, a lad in khakis (boot cut) says,
I've got 4,000 followers. You're
joking, right? another
      replies, I've got two-times that.
Ka-ching.
Let me in. lululemon
      And Life Time are both fans.
Mixed lots. Marketing plots.
      Maybe we should peg funds
      for a podcast spot, if
not this year, then next
      nodded the nearest blazer
      licking rose-colored icing,
Opportunities, both covert and
      overt—lots
Perhaps the pink bowties aren't enough
Quiet, another says. I've had my share
      of pastel-dyed stuff

Right / Righteous / Rightfulness-not, think the ghosts in the room,
      eying glasses of water. Wishing

and willing to splash the diluted,
tepid liquids on the gel-covered heads
Cynicism and capitalism persist
in all corners
Sorry, not sorry, to interrupt, are we good?
the moderator and minute-taker asks
I've got back-to-backs
Today. Tomorrow, too.
All talk of Dilbert squandered
Updates and alerts proliferate
Umpire, usurp, and underemployed - both nouns and verbs, as
vast inequities—pay/education/employment—persist
STEM versus STEAM debates boil, yet
women remain three times as likely to be asked
to make hot drinks at work
Women do the work and neither wait nor wonder
yet Scott Adams makes headlines
Where's the coverage of
Sadie L.,
Mary Newbury,
Pauline, and Abigail Smith
Adams (and others)—and
what about the other 364 days
and the infinite ways
inequality persists
in pay gaps and platitudes
Unproductive claims on reproductive rights
sexist jokes and teams called woke
Uncompensated labor and overcompensated male behavior
Elections, board rooms, call for peace (square) tables
Mandatory yes ma'ams and pat-the-back slaps
are laundered, pressed, and delivered
xtra emphasis on all bumpers

You can do it all, high-gloss stickers say
When divided labor should be the way
Zeus and gods of work remain woefully out of order

A Bingo Board Reflection on International Women's Day (IWD)

With acronyms, pay grades, and awarded letters (STEM, STEAM, and more) persistently out of order, and boardrooms as much games of bingo and inside lingo (single syllables were his name-o), we anticipate International Women's Day with a blend (savory, not necessarily sweet) of history and forward-focused wordplay. Amidst a mixed lot heavy of marketing plots, we parse the phrases and highlight the persistent flops, often gaping. Stop the groping. Cease the claims of irreverent poking and deeply questionable marketing. Co-opting in plain sight. We seek transparency, with no more Hide-and-Go-Seek. We stake a rightful seat at all tables. We mark the board in ways neither cobbled not stereotypically labeled. We are always able.

Ready. Set. Play.

Pins a blend of kitsch and retro parade on public transportation	Email bait suggests access to capital, when in reality it's just another marketing game (capitalized and co-opted)	"You Can Do It All" Stickers, $10 a pack	A job description with an inadvertent "he" in the preferred qualifications	Confusion over official International Women's Day and UN themes

Rosie the Riveter impersonators kvetch on AM radio	A half dozen pink cupcakes with purple, green, and white sprinkles (decorations designed to please) sell at six for a dollar, all home-baked by female staffers after hours	IWD social media post typo—swapping stranger for stronger	Fight songs and claims of nastiness play on conservative radio	Random guy on YouTube debates strength's form of speech. Notes on appearance proliferate in the Comments, along with quotes: 'Unlike women, strength is neither a noun nor a verb."
Tied up in meetings, by the time you made it to the company-sponsored celebration, no food or drink remained. Clean-up crew? a stranger asks.	Gmail Calendar Alert: Office IWD Celebration and School Pick-Up conflict	A chap in a pre-shrunk "Women Crush Everyday" T-Shirt blows smoke and holds a can of Orange Crush at a red light. All engines in reverse.	A pastel polka dot bowtie spotted in a parade of hot-pink SukiShufu Lycra Leggings	Men in 'Women Matter" themed T-shirts on TV debate the overturning of Roe v. Wade

Corporate posts drafted and signed by ChatGPT	Five invites, all for no pay, to panels that lack any diversity. Questions— are they paying you to attend, plan, speak— left unsaid.	Males pat each other on the back as they celebrate the success of their latest corporate campaign for women's rights	IWD fundraiser, all items homemade by women staff, for free	Scott Adams gets more airtime, while Sadie L., Mary Newbury, Pauline, and Abigail Smith Adams (and others)get no mention
Sexist jokes posted in a monitored chat during a Zoom webinar promoting female staff	"Feminist AF" bits on FM Radio	"Strong Women Stay" tweets fill X (formerly known as Twitter) timelines alongside urgings to flee	At a speaker panel table with Sylvia Pankhurst pin giveaways, a dude asks for an extra guest pass (free, please)	Power suits, on sale. 50% off

"Advice from a Caterpillar" (on freedom)

(to be)

free at last!

a tone of delight
another moment,
a sea
distant green leaves

    wandering
    in a hurry
    alone!

    sleep
    the highest tree
    in the wood

    free ... at last

what are you?

invent something!

    an egg!

Glossary

Identity of a Suffragist / an Incomplete (and Under-Studied)
Glossary of Terms (and Leading Ladies)

1. Alice
—an appropriate first name for suffragists seeking new (wonder)
lands. Popularized in the Victorian Era and at the turn of century,
the name clarified that even the most traditional families knew
there might be novel opportunities for women far beyond (and
through) the looking glass

2. Bill
—neither a brother nor a barrister; a piece of legislative material; a
hill (to climb) in the name of a better tomorrow

3. Canvas
—a representative fabric, fit to a people flawed but committed to
stretch and stitch new patterns of reform

4. Do
—a demarcation for a series of deeds (not words), documents
(signed proclamations), and declarations (the state of a new
nation). *Do not beg. Do not grovel. Do not fear.*

5. Formed Discontent
—frustration-fueled feminism or feminism-fueled frustration

6. Height
—a deceptively complex heuristic woven of fishnets, slights, and
persistent fight (might)

7. Latitude and Longitude
—complexion points where grit tangoes with gripes

8. Monarchs
—of unclipped wings and far-flung swings

9. Noun
—how a girl should regard themself (preferred to an adjective).
Attribution: Elizabeth Cady Stanton

10. Pocket
—a preparedness pouch for punches, predictions, and premonitions

11. Rash
—passion patch

12. Sash
—stabilizing force

13. Sisterhood
—a fashion statement

14. Suffix
—suffragists and suffragettes share more similarities than differences

15. Sworn Testimony
—swords of truth. servings of time

16. To Flag
—verb: make waves. make wind. make way

17. Work for Women
—an ongoing process

18. You
    —*the change-maker between Amendments 18 and 19*

Notes

[7] "my head's free at last"
Found in *Alice in Wonderland*, Chapter 5

[16] "on defining a movement :: of freedom and liberty"
<https://www.nps.gov/people/judith-winsor-smith.htm>

[50] "Josephine Butler / To Lift the 'Fallen Women'"
<https://artsandculture.google.com/story/sexual-
revolutionaries-of-the-suffrage-movement-lse-library/
zQXBb13WOTDcIQ?hl=en>

[51] "A Woman Named Josephine"
<https://artsandculture.google.com/story/sexual-
revolutionaries-of-the-suffrage-movement-lse-library/
zQXBb13WOTDcIQ?hl=en>

[56] "She's Got Legs"
<https://www.britannica.com/biography/Amelia-Bloomer>

[63] "Travel Costs"
Historical Statistics of the United States, Colonial Times to 1970
(Washington: U.S. Government Printing Office, 1975; HA202.B87
1975 MRR Ref Desk and other locations), 1: 168.   <https://guides.
loc.gov/american-women-essays/marching-for-the-vote#note20>

[64] "I Followed Him"
<https://readingpalawyer.com/a-peek-into-the-archives-reveals-
womens-suffrage-as-a-cause-for-divorce>

[77] "As a Child"
<https://timesmachine.nytimes.com/
timesmachine/1913/11/22/100288542.pdf?pdf_
redirect=true&ip=0>   <https://www.nytimes.com/1897/01/03/
archives/do-women-hate-women-a-man-says-that-they-do-but-
three-women-say-not.html>

[80] "a woman named Alice: inventor of _____"
<https://www.teachingcalifornia.org/resource/alice_
paul_describes_force_feeding> <https://www.nytimes.
com/1913/11/22/archives/lucy-burns-fined-1-militant-proudly-
pays-for-chalking-the-white.html>

[81] "A Jiu-Jitsu Artist's Dream"
<https://poets.org/poem/why-we-oppose-pockets-women>

[86] "ascensor :: together we lift"
<https://www.history.com/news/night-terror-brutality-
suffragists-19th-amendment> <https://books.google.com/
books?id=3eQm9wZIMEkC&printsec=frontcover&source=gbs_
ge_summary_r&cad=0#v=onepage&q&f=false> <https://www.
pbs.org/wgbh/americanexperience/features/wilson-womens-
suffrage>

[112] "Dear Alice"
<https://poets.org/poem/why-we-oppose-pockets-women>

[118] "How It Feels: On the Issue of Women's Suffrage"
<https://www.degruyter.com/document/
doi/10.4159/9780674240797-011/html?lang=en>
Citation: Ware, Susan. "How It Feels to Be the Husband of a
Suffragette," *Why They Marched: Untold Stories of the Women Who
Fought for the Right to Vote*. Cambridge, Massachusetts, and London,
England: Harvard University Press, 2019, pp. 137–150. https://
doi.org/10.4159/9780674240797-011.   Found by skimming the
description of the events surrounding a visit from British suffragist
Emmeline Pankhurst to Harvard University. Repurposed language
initially used to describe the tactical negotiations and maneuvers
that accompanied the visit to instead highlight the unspoken shifts
such negotiations promoted and promoted.

[119] "How to Be: The Husband of a Suffragette"
<https://www.degruyter.com/document/
doi/10.36019/9780813550756-041/html>

[120] "To (Be a) Witness: Found in the Clerk's Report Transport"
Found in "Witness Payment Report in U.S. vs. Susan B. Anthony";
<https://www.docsteach.org/documents/document/anthony-
payment-report> Witnesses for the case U.S. vs. Susan B.
Anthony were recorded and amounts due were tallied. The
transcript in which this piece was found was a tally of refunds due
for travel based on days of court attendance and miles traveled.

[121] "A Woman Indicted"
Illustrative Source (Sample Indictment, One of Many of
the Female Sex); <https://www.docsteach.org/documents/
document/chatfield-indictment-order> For more indictments,
the National Archives maintains multiple records of Federal Court
indictments for women arrested for illegally voting in the 1872
election in Rochester, New York.

[122] "How to [confuse] Incite a Citizenry: In Plain Sight"
<https://www.docsteach.org/documents/document/anthony-
indictment> A compilation and remix of transcript titles and
lines found in June 1873 transcripts.

[123] "An Abecedarian on International Women's Day"
<https://www.linkedin.com/pulse/corporate-problem-
international-womens-day-ebony-breen?trk=articles_directory>
<https://www.weforum.org/agenda/2023/02/international-
women-day-what-why-when> <https://www.bbc.com/news/
world-64723201>

Jen Schneider is an award-winning author, essayist, and educator who lives, writes, and works in small spaces throughout Pennsylvania (though she mostly spends her days on West Coast time). She writes poetry, non-fiction, fiction, and creative non-fiction, with an emphasis on (and soft spot for) interactive and hybrid forms. She especially enjoys focusing on lesser-known voices in history and spotlighting the work of women and history in her writing. She has authored several chapbooks and full-length poetry collections, with stories, poems, and essays published through traditional and independent presses and in a variety of literary and scholarly journals. Previous works include *Invisible Ink; On Habits & Habitats; On Daily Puzzles: (Un)locking Invisibility; A Collection of Recollections; When Links / Blanks / Puzzles Linger; On Always Being an Outsider; Blindfolds, Bruises, and Breakups; 14 (Plus) Reasons Why; To Wish to Walk,* and On *(Pantry) Stock & (Kitchen) Timers.* She served as the 2022 Montgomery County (PA) Poet Laureate.

SHANTI ARTS

NATURE • ART • SPIRIT

Please visit us online
to browse our entire book catalog,
including poetry collections and fiction,
books on travel, nature, healing, art,
photography, and more.

Also take a look at our highly regarded art
and literary journal, *Still Point Arts Quarterly*,
which may be downloaded for free.

www.shantiarts.com

www.ingramcontent.com/pod-product-compliance
Lightning Source LLC
Chambersburg PA
CBHW032055090426
42744CB00005B/225